This Book Belongs To:

_____

_____

_____

Rome
ITALY

Hamburg, Germany

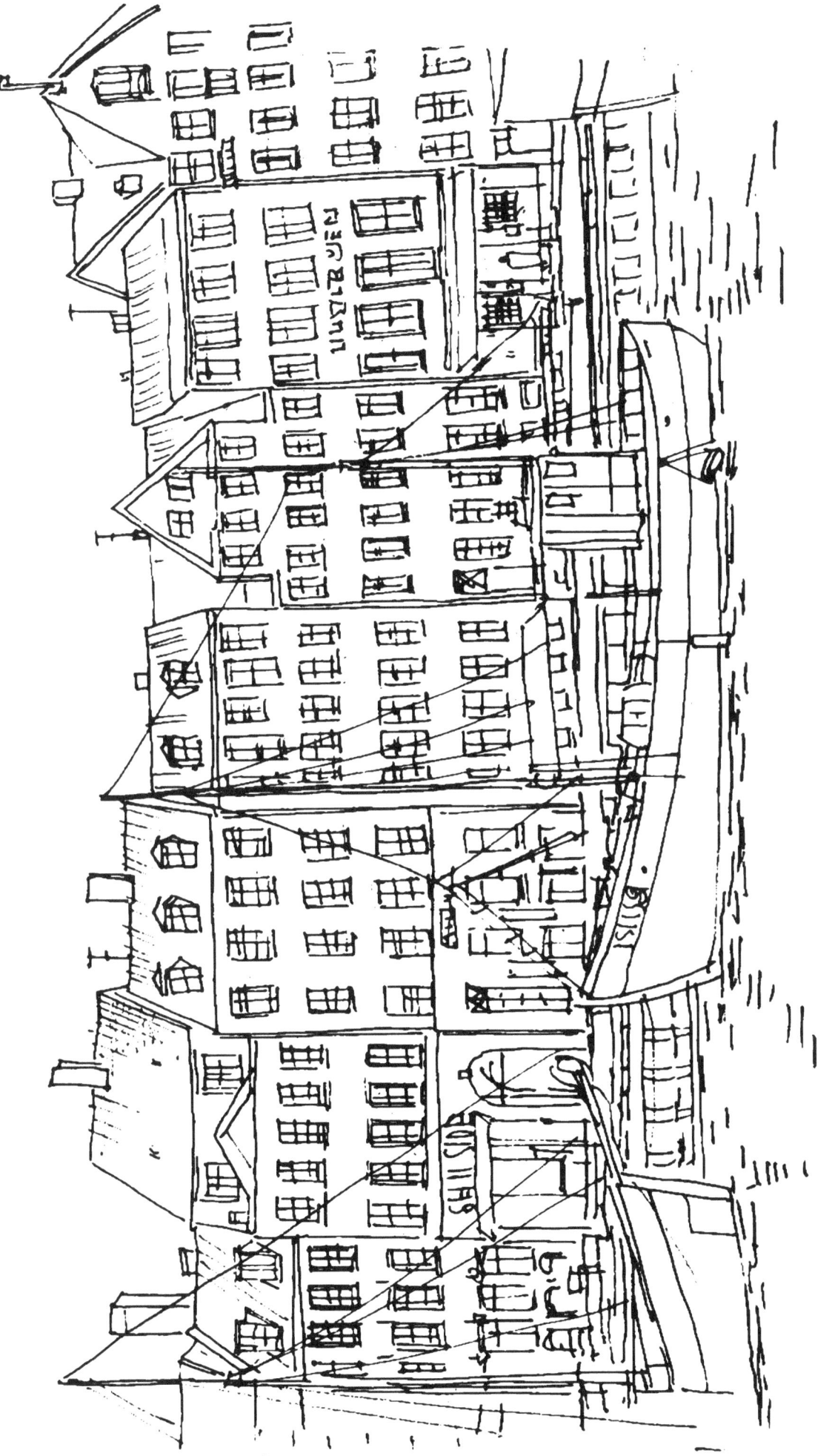

COPENHAGEN
Denmark

SAINT PETERSBURG
Russia

ISTANBUL
Turkey

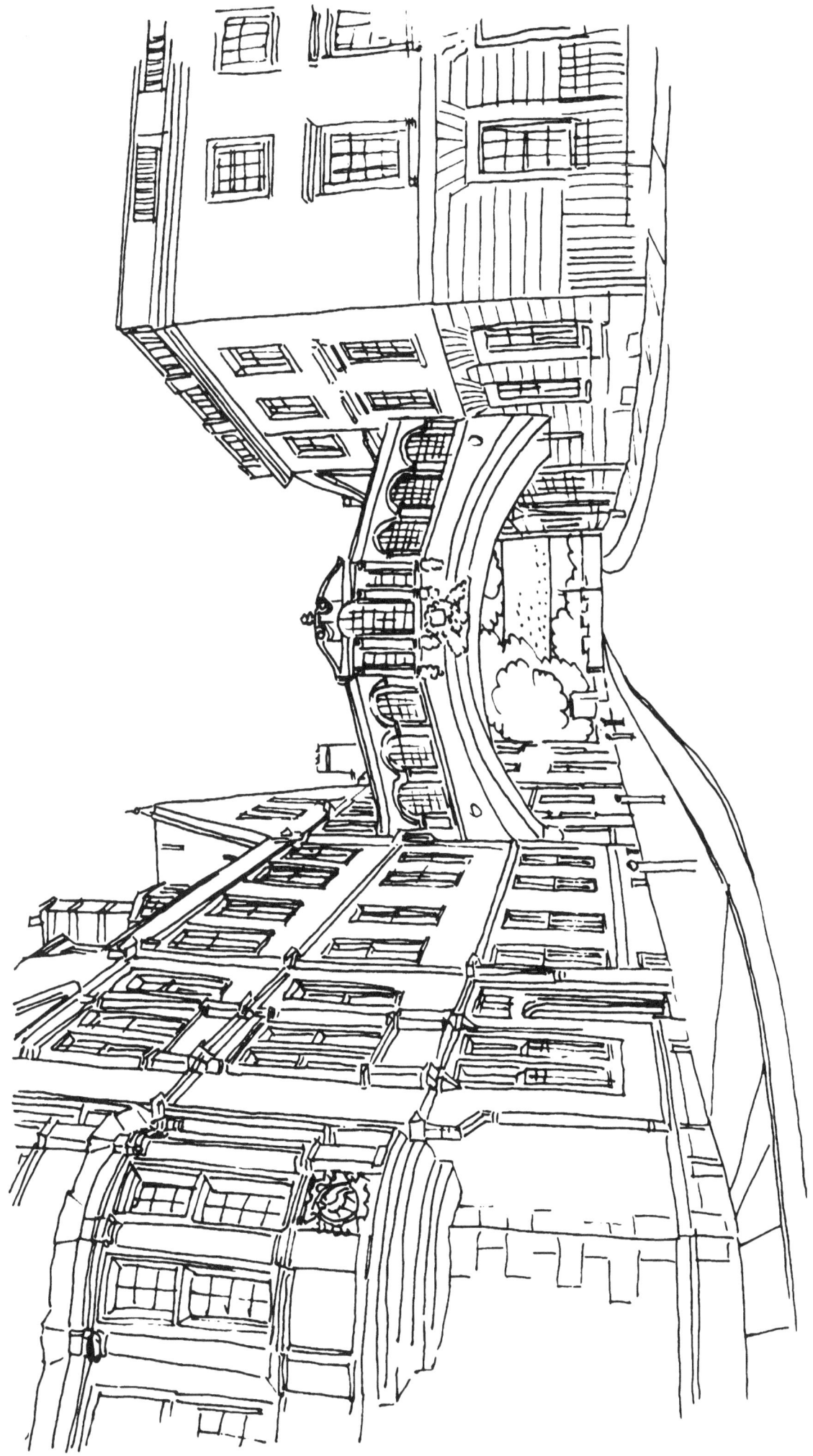

OXFORD, UNITED KINGDOM

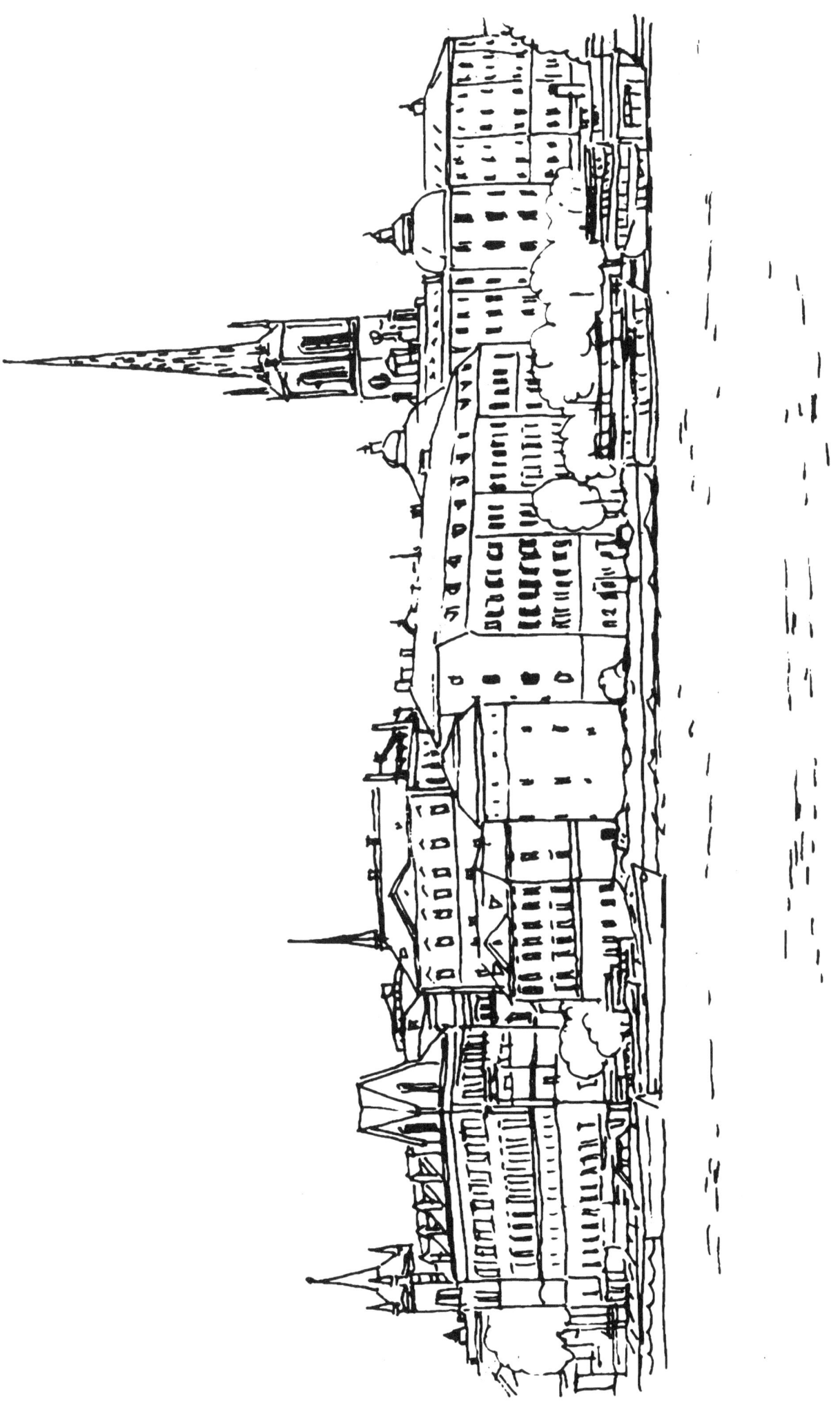

Paris, France

Taipei, Taiwan

Vienna, Austria

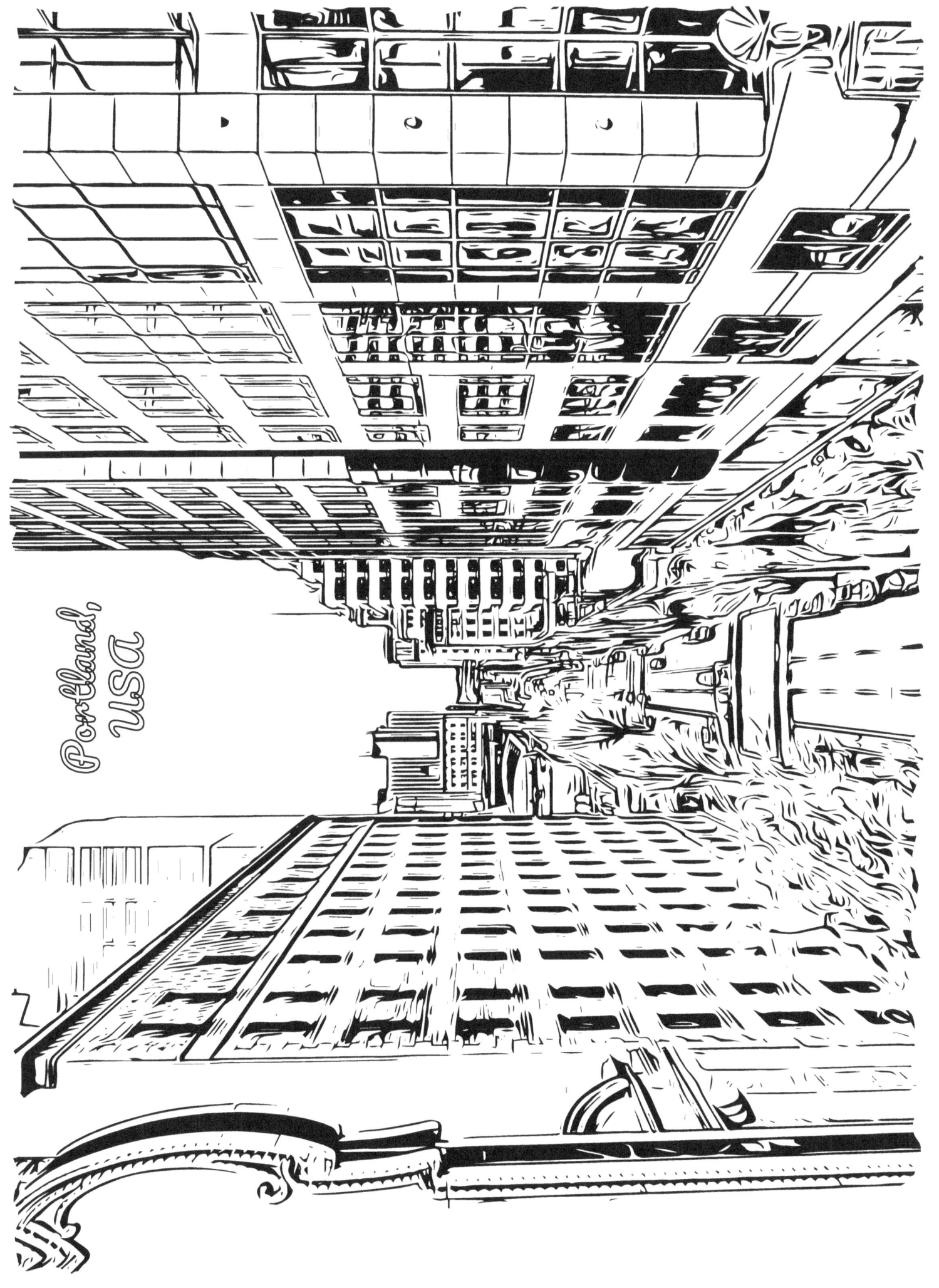

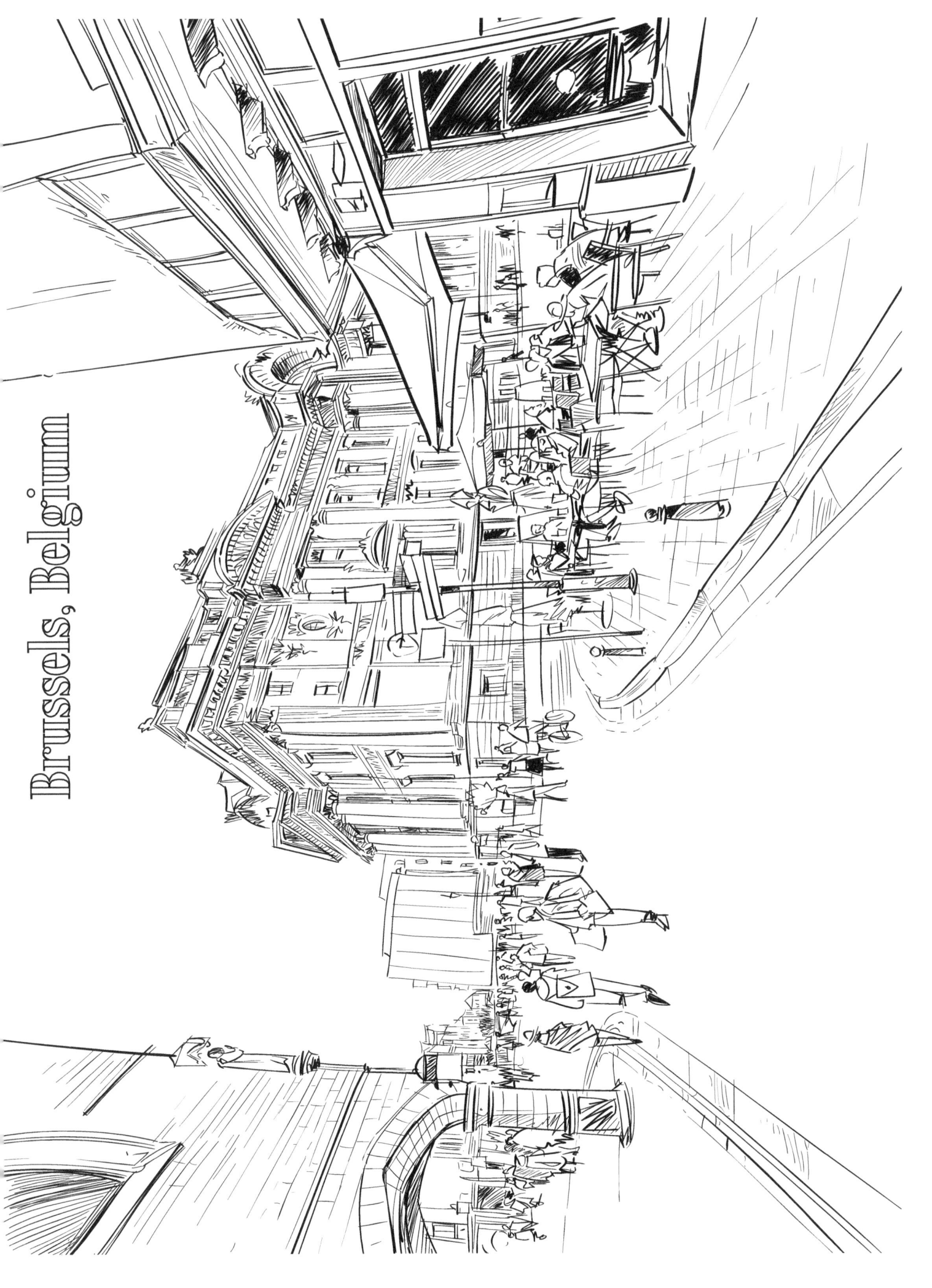

Krakow, Poland

Paris, France

Budapest, Hungary

Moscow, Russia

Lyon, France

Dubai. United Arab Emirates

Dresden, Germany

Barcelona, Spain

Thank you for your purchase and we hope you enjoyed our book!

Your feedback is greatly appreciated as it lets us know how we are doing!

For all inquiries, email us at groenambrosiapress@gmail.com